AN UNOFFICIAL ACTIVITY BOOK

VOCABULARY
FOR
MINECRAFTERS

ACTIVITIES TO HELP KIDS BOOST
READING AND LANGUAGE SKILLS

Grades 1-2

Sky Pony Press
New York, New York

Copyright © 2022 by Hollan Publishing, Inc.

Minecraft® is a registered trademark of Notch Development AB.

The Minecraft game is copyright © Mojang AB.

Sky Pony Press books may be purchased in bulk at special discounts for sales promotion, corporate gifts, fund-raising, or educational purposes. Special editions can also be created to specifications. For details, contact the Special Sales Department, Sky Pony Press, 307 West 36th Street, 11th Floor, New York, NY 10018 or info@skyhorsepublishing.com.

Sky Pony® is a registered trademark of Skyhorse Publishing, Inc.®, a Delaware corporation.

Visit our website at www.skyhorsepublishing.com.

10 9 8 7 6 5 4 3 2 1

Library of Congress Cataloging-in-Publication Data is available on file.

Cover and interior illustration by Grace Sandford

Book design by Noora Cox

Print ISBN: 978-1-5107-7109-3

Printed in China

A NOTE TO PARENTS

Build their vocabulary, one fun activity at a time!

When you want to reinforce classroom skills at home, it's crucial to have kid-friendly learning materials. This *Vocabulary for Minecrafters* workbook transforms language development into an irresistible adventure complete with diamond swords, zombies, skeletons, and ghasts.

Vocabulary for Minecrafters is also fully aligned with National Common Core Standards for 1st and 2nd English Language Arts (ELA). Encourage your child to progress at his or her own pace. Learning is best when students are challenged, but not frustrated. What's most important is that your Minecrafter is engaged in his or her own learning.

With more than 50 gamer-friendly practice pages, puzzles, and familiar Minecraft characters on every page, your child will be eager to dive in and level up their reading and vocabulary skills.

Happy adventuring!

COMMON NOUNS

A noun is a person, a place, or thing. Look at the nouns below. Write them in the correct column on the chart.

~~Alex~~   apple   Steve

flower   Overworld   emerald

Nether   villager   pickaxe

PERSON	PLACE	THING
Alex		

NUMBER WORDS

Look at this player's inventory. Spell out the number of each item. Use the word box for help.

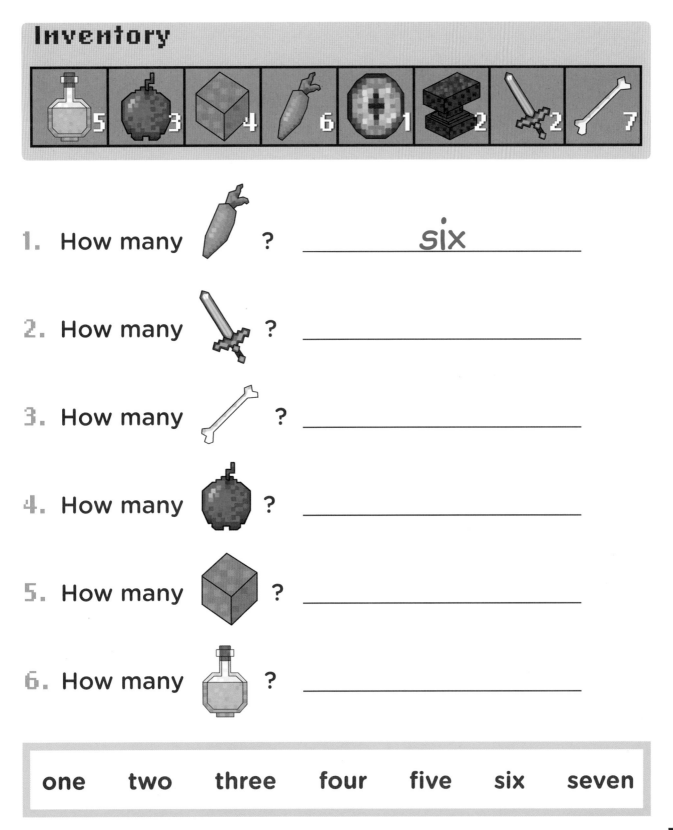

Inventory

5	3	4	6	1	2	2	7

1. How many ? __six__

2. How many ? _____

3. How many ? _____

4. How many ? _____

5. How many ? _____

6. How many ? _____

one	two	three	four	five	six	seven

DESCRIBING WORDS

Use an adjective from the box to finish the sentence.

spotted	~~loud~~	fast	diamond	boss	tamed

1. The ghast makes a _____ loud _____ sound.

2. Potion of Swiftness makes me very _____ .

3. Look at my _____ spawn egg!

4. I crafted a _____ sword.

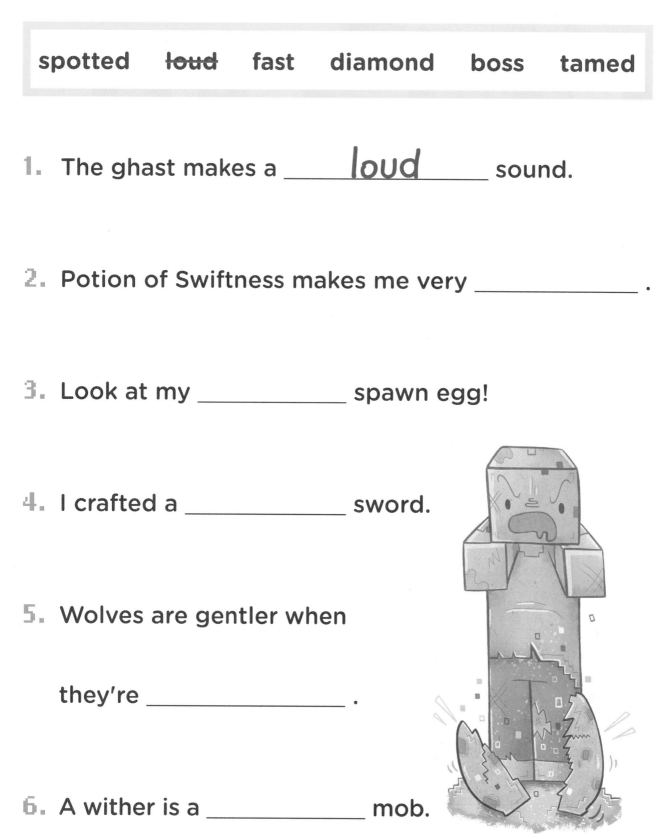

5. Wolves are gentler when

    they're _____ .

6. A wither is a _____ mob.

SYNONYMS

Synonyms are words that mean almost the same thing. Finish the sentence using any of the three synonyms provided.

1. That baby panda is _____cute_____ .
   (adorable, cute, lovable)

2. The Ender dragon is _____ .
   (scary, frightening, fearsome)

3. The sound a ghast makes is _____ .
   (creepy, spooky, eerie)

4. Awkward potion is _____ for making other potions.   (useful, helpful, handy)

Write three **synonyms** that describe this GIANT zombie:

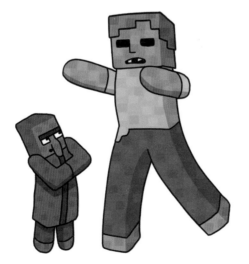

_____   _____   _____

QUESTION WORDS

Use one of the question words to fill in the blank.

What   **When**   ~~**Where**~~   **Why**   **How**

1. **QUESTION:** <u>Where</u> does the witch live?
   ANSWER: The witch lives in a swamp hut.

2. **QUESTION:** _____ color is an Enderman?
   ANSWER: It is black.

3. **QUESTION:** _____ do you break a block?
   ANSWER: You break it with a pickaxe.

4. **QUESTION:** _____ does it get dark?
   ANSWER: It gets dark at night.

5. **QUESTION:** _____ do people play Minecraft
   ANSWER: It's fun!

Now write your own question about Minecraft. Start with a word from the word box. Read it to someone and see if they know the answer!

_____

CROSSWORD FOR CRAFTERS

Sight words are words that appear many times in the books you read. Learn them and reading will be easier! Read the sight words and write them in the puzzle.

ACROSS

1 ~~are~~
2 for
3 was
4 that
6 the
7 you

DOWN

1 and
3 with
5 they

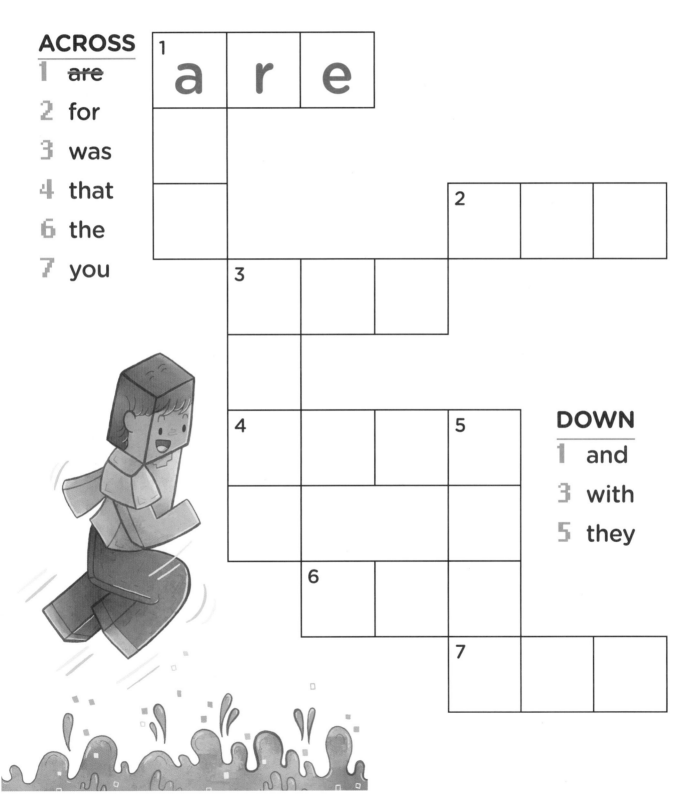

1 a r e

MATH WORD MAKER

Unscramble the math words below.

add	equal	length	~~measure~~
sum	subtract	weight	shape

1. aeusrem _measure_

2. giweth _____

3. dad _____

4. msu _____

5. laque _____

6. battrusc _____

7. hasep _____

8. ghelnt _____

THE POWER OF PREFIXES

A **prefix** is a letter or group of letters that go in front of a word and change the meaning of the word.

> **re-** *means "again"*
>
> **un-** *means "not"*

Fill in the chart by adding the prefix to the root word. Then explain the meaning of the new word.

ROOT WORD	PREFIX	NEW WORD	MEANING
happy	un-	unhappy	not happy
play	re-		
true	un-		
do	re-		
lucky	un-		
read	re-		

DESCRIBING WORDS

An **adverb** is a word that describes a verb or an adjective to make it more interesting. Use an adverb from the box to finish the sentence.

quickly	~~quietly~~	loudly	slowly	gently	happily

1. Steve hides _____ quietly _____ behind the tree.

2. The turtle moves _____ on land.

3. Potion of Swiftness makes him

   move _____ .

4. The kids played _____
   for hours.

5. The Zombie approached the villager

   moaning _____ .

6. The tamed cat took the fish _____
   from Alex's hand.

POSSESSIVE PRONOUNS

A **possessive pronoun** is a word that shows ownership. Fill in the blank with a possessive pronoun from the word box.

mine	yours	his	~~hers~~	theirs	ours

1. The sword belongs to the girl.

   The sword is _____ hers _____ .

2. The hut belongs to the witches.

   The hut is _____ .

3. The crafting table belongs to you.

   The table is _____ .

4. The Potion of Swiftness belongs to the boy.

   The potion is _____ .

5. The gold ingots belong to me.

   The ingots are _____ .

6. The farm belongs to us.

   The farm is _____ .

SIGHT WORD SEARCH

Sight words are words that appear many times in the books you read. Learn them and reading will be easier! Find the words in the word search puzzle.

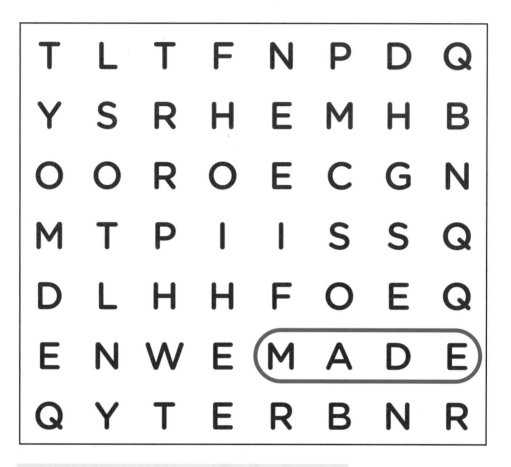

T L T F N P D Q
Y S R H E M H B
O O R O E C G N
M T P I I S S Q
D L H H F O E Q
E N W E M A D E
Q Y T E R B N R

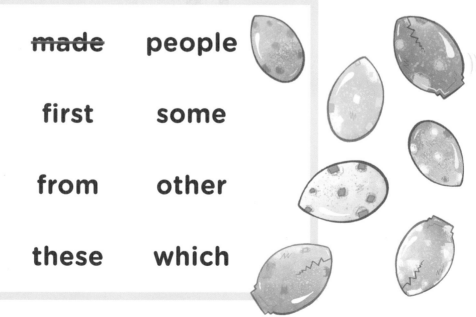

~~made~~   people

first   some

from   other

these   which

SCIENCE WORD SCRAMBLE

Unscramble the science words below. Use the words in the word box to help you.

energy	pattern	earth	plant
sound	~~oil~~	moon	system

1. lio _____oil_____

2. onom _____

3. genrye _____

4. htera _____

5. ltpan _____

6. trnepta _____

7. nudso _____

8. ymsset _____

PLURAL NOUNS

To make some nouns **plural**, you need to change the ending **-y** to **-ies**. Match the singular word in the left column to the plural form in the right column.

SINGULAR   **PLURAL**

1. baby   butterflies

2. butterfly   tries

3. try   lilies

4. city   parties

5. party   babies

6. lily   studies

7. study   cities

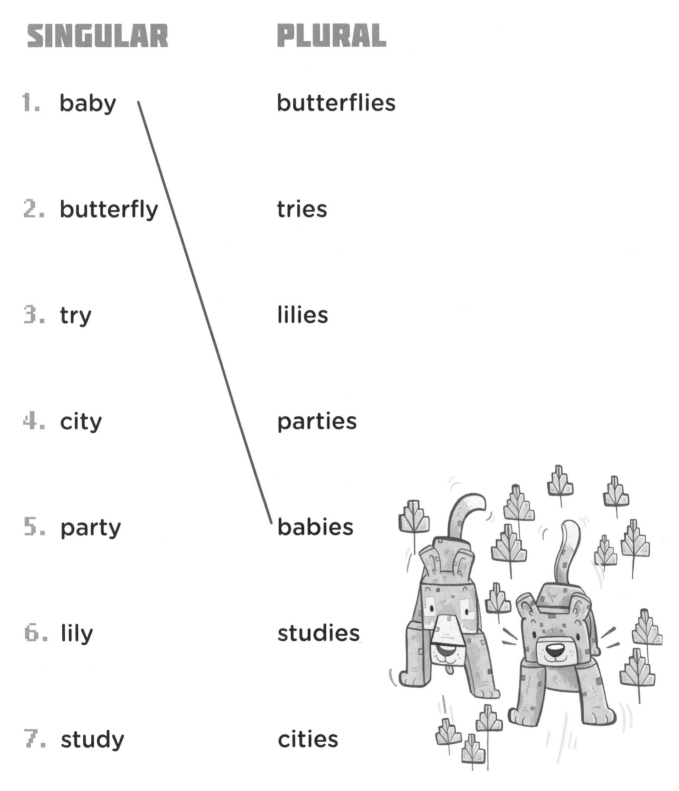

REGULAR PAST TENSE

The **past tense** tells that an action has already happened. The verbs in the chart are *regular*, meaning to make them past tense you add *-ed*. Change each regular verb to past tense.

BASE FORM	PAST TENSE
call	called
teleport	
chase	
mine	
attack	
plant	

IRREGULAR PAST TENSE

The **past tense** tells that an action has already happened. Some verbs are *irregular,* meaning they are *not* formed by adding *-ed*. These words you just have to know. Change each irregular verb to past tense.

BASE FORM	PAST TENSE
sit	*sat*
hide	
tell	
sleep	
make	
get	
fight	

CROSSWORD FOR CRAFTERS

Sight words are words that appear many times in the books you read. Learn them and reading will be easier! Use the sight words in the box and the clues to finish the puzzle.

long	people	words	before
look	water	great	name

(~~long~~)

DOWN

1 Something you do with your eyes

3 Better than good

4 Opposite of after

7 What you are called

ACROSS

2 Opposite of short

5 More than one person

6 What a sentence is made of

8 Something you drink

2 l o n g

NOUNS, ADJECTIVES, AND VERBS

A noun is a person, place, or thing. Underline the **nouns** in each sentence below.

1. The <u>player</u> spawns the <u>skeleton</u>.

2. In his hand is a pickaxe.

Adjectives are describing words. Circle the **adjective** in each sentence below.

3. The gamer wears gold armor.

4. The player has a diamond pickaxe.

A verb is an action word. Draw a box around the **verb** in each sentence below.

5. The player inspects the spawner cage.

6. The skeleton looks scared.

Write your own sentence about the picture using a **noun**, an **adjective**, and a **verb**.

7. _____ .

SORT THE WORDS

Sort the words in the word box into the correct category in the chart.

~~pants~~	green
purple	coat
orange	blue
shirt	white
shoes	scarf

COLOR

CLOTHING

pants

LANGUAGE ARTS WORD SCRAMBLE

Unscramble the language arts words below. Use the words in the word box to help you.

author   capital   ~~draft~~   letter
period   revise   sentence

1. fradt _____ *draft* _____

2. idepro _____

3. trleet _____

4. enstcnee _____

5. tacpial _____

6. ersvei _____

7. uraoht _____

FUTURE TENSE

Add *will* before a verb to indicate that the action will happen in the future. Change the verb in the chart to the future tense.

BASE FORM	FUTURE TENSE
see	*will see*
use	
craft	
get	
chop	
build	

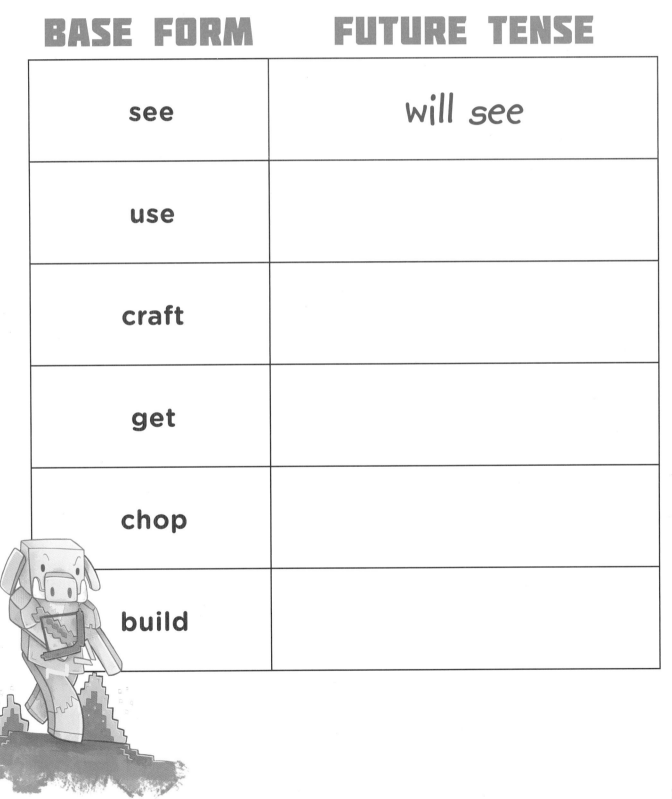

IRREGULAR PAST TENSE VERBS

Use the words from the box to write the past tense of the verb in the sentence.

had	made	said	~~was~~
did	wrote	were	

1. Alex _____was_____ fighting the Ender dragon.
   (is)

2. Steve _____ what he could to win the battle.
   (do)

3. The witch _____ a special potion.
   (has)

4. She _____ gold armor using her crafting table.
   (make)

5. The villager _____ he would trade me for emeralds. (say)

6. The ghasts _____ screeching.
   (are)

7. The girl _____ a story about Minecraft.
   (write)

IRREGULAR PLURAL NOUNS

Circle the correct irregular plural form of each noun.

1. tooth

a. tooths　　(b. teeth)

2. woman

a. women　　b. womans

3. foot

a. foots　　b. feet

4. child

a. childs　　b. children

5. mouse

a. mice　　b. mouses

6. fish

a. fish　　b. fishes

SUPER SUFFIXES

A **suffix** is a letter or group of letters that go at the end of a word and change the meaning of the word.

-ful   *means "full of"*

-or   *means "a person who"*

Fill in the chart by adding the suffix to the root word. Then explain the meaning of the new word.

ROOT WORD	PREFIX	NEW WORD	MEANING
joy	-ful	joyful	full of joy
act	-or		
fear	-ful		
edit	-or		
hope	-ful		
sail	-or		

ADD AN ADJECTIVE

Adjectives describe nouns and make them more specific. Compare these two sentences:

The witch made the potion.

*The witch made the **fizzy** potion.*

For each underlined noun, think of an adjective to describe it and write it on the line.

1. The zombie wears _____iron_____ armor.

2. The ghast makes _____ noises.

3. The Ender dragon has a/an _____ tail.

4. She entered the _____ cave.

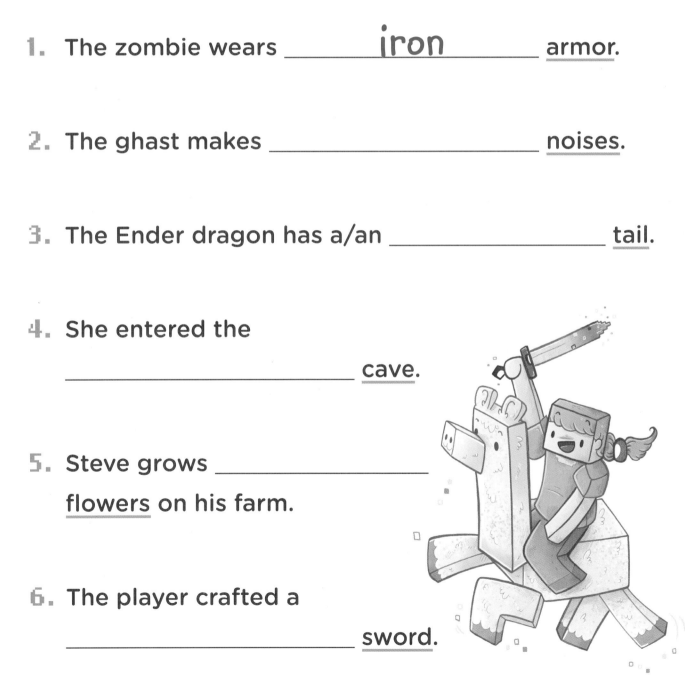

5. Steve grows _____ flowers on his farm.

6. The player crafted a _____ sword.

ADD AN ADVERB

Adverbs describe an action and make sentences more interesting. Compare these two sentences:

"We won the game," they shouted.

*"We won the game," they shouted **happily**.*

Add an adverb from the word box to describe each underlined verb.

~~bravely~~	neatly	loudly
sadly	very	easily

1. The player <u>fought</u> _____**bravely**_____ against the giant iron golem.

2. Alex was _____ <u>lucky</u> to find diamonds.

3. Steve used a map so he could _____ <u>find</u> his way.

4. "I lost my dog," she <u>said</u> _____ .

5. The crops were <u>planted</u> _____ in rows.

6. The wither <u>screeched</u> _____ at the players.

SOCIAL STUDIES WORD SCRAMBLE

Unscramble the social studies words below. Use the words in the word box to help you.

family	~~culture~~	globe	map
belief	symbol	history	value

1. luctuer _____ culture _____

2. pam _____

3. bleog _____

4. maliyf _____

5. tioyrhs _____

6. eluva _____

7. fliebe _____

8. mbyslo _____

SORT THE WORDS

Sort the words in the word box into the correct category in the chart.

~~dog~~	nine
three	bat
squid	ten
fish	cat
seven	eight

ANIMAL  NUMBER

dog

SIGHT WORD SEARCH

Sight words are words that appear many times in the books you read. Learn them and reading will be easier! Find the words in the word search puzzle.

~~house~~	very
came	world
thing	would
through	some

PLURAL NOUNS

Add **-s** or **-es** to make each noun plural.

SINGULAR	PLURAL
fence	fences
fox	
ender pearl	
block	
llama	
bush	
ladder	
compass	

FREQUENTLY CONFUSED WORDS

Some words sound the same but are spelled differently and mean different things. The words in parentheses are often confused for each other. Write the correct word on the line to complete the sentence.

1. The kids play _____**their**_____ game.
   (their, they're, there)

2. Steve shot _____ arrows.
   (too, two, to)

3. The Minecraft music is so loud I can't _____ you.
   (hear, here)

4. The griefer looted _____ chest of items!
   (your, you're)

5. The cave spider spun _____ web.
   (it's, its)

6. The Potion of Water Breathing _____ you breathe underwater.
   (lets, let's)

SIGHT WORD OPPOSITES

Match each **sight word** in the left column with its opposite meaning in the right column.

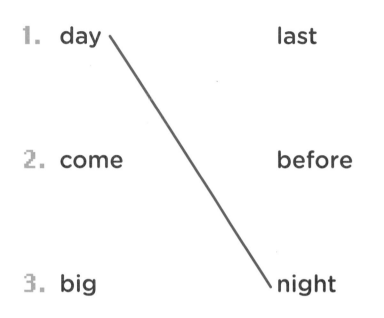

1. day   last

2. come   before

3. big   night

4. first   go

5. after   answer

6. question   follow

7. lead   small

IRREGULAR PAST TENSE

The **past tense** tells that an action has already happened. Some verbs are *irregular*, meaning they are *not* formed by adding *-ed*. These words you just have to know. Change the irregular verb in the chart to the past tense.

PRESENT TENSE	PAST TENSE
catch	caught
sleep	
begin	
come	
say	
see	

COMMONLY CONFUSED WORDS

Some words sound the same but are spelled differently and mean different things. The words in parentheses are often confused for each other. Write the correct word on the line to complete the sentence.

1. ___**Are**___ we playing Minecraft today?
   (our, are)

2. I have _____ exploring the Overworld.
   (been, bin)

3. Let's _____ new skins for Minecraft.
   (buy, by)

4. The player _____ how to craft a Potion of Healing.   *(new, knew)*

5. The dolphin likes to swim in the _____ .
   (sea, see)

6. You made a _____ shot with your bow and arrow!   *(grate, great)*

7. There are _____ hostile mobs coming after us.   *(no, know)*

MATH WORD MAKER

Unscramble the math words below.

round	double	whole	value
digit	~~zero~~	graph	minus

1. ozer _____zero_____

2. smiun _____

3. lwoeh _____

4. hrgap _____

5. obdleu _____

6. uleva _____

7. druno _____

8. itidg _____

CROSSWORD FOR CRAFTERS

Sight words are words that appear many times in the books you read. Learn them and reading will be easier! Use the sight words in the box and the clues to finish the puzzle.

| ~~world~~ | air | many | learn |
| find | because | now | time |

4 Across: w o r l d

ACROSS

4 Another word for globe

6 Opposite of few

7 Answer to why

8 Opposite of search

DOWN

1 Opposite of later

2 What you breathe

3 What a clock tells you

5 What you do in school

ROOT WORDS

A **root word** does not have a prefix or a suffix. It is the basic part of a word and has its own meaning. Underline the root word in the examples below. Then separate the word into its two parts.

1. <u>mad</u>ness

   _____mad_____   _____ness_____

2. undone

   _____   _____

3. timeless

   _____   _____

4. useful

   _____   _____

5. teacher

   _____   _____

6. remove

   _____   _____

7. return

   _____   _____

8. learner

   _____   _____

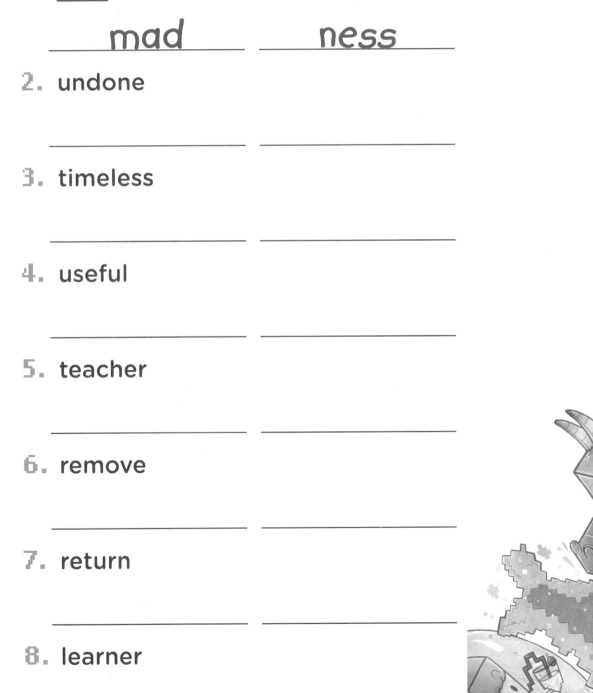

FILL-IN-THE-BLANK STORY

Use the words in the word box to make a fun story about Minecraft.

| ship | green | ~~help~~ | lead |
| see | smart | feed | chest |

A dolphin can _____ help _____ you find buried

treasure. First, you have to _____ it

raw fish. Then the dolphin will _____ you

to a sunken _____ . Inside that old boat

is a treasure _____ . Open it up to

_____ what is inside!

Sometimes you will get many

_____ emeralds. It is

good to have a _____

animal like a dolphin to help you.

MATCH THE SUBJECT AND VERB

Fill in the chart with the correct form of the verb.

BASE FORM	SHE OR HE	THEY	I	YOU
hop	hops	hop	hop	hop
write				
help				
live				
read				

COMPOUND WORDS

Compound words combine two single words into a new word. Combine the two words shown in the chart to make a new word.

bed	+	time	=	*bedtime*
row	+	boat	=	
back	+	pack	=	
bird	+	house	=	
note	+	book	=	
book	+	mark	=	
class	+	room	=	

COLLECTIVE NOUNS

A **collective noun** is a name for a collection of people, animals, or things. A *team* is made up of single *players*, but we talk about the team as the whole group.

Match the single nouns on the left to the collective noun on the right.

1. flowers   stack

2. birds   group

3. soldiers   flock

4. friends   school

5. books   choir

6. singers   bouquet

7. fish   band

8. musicians   army

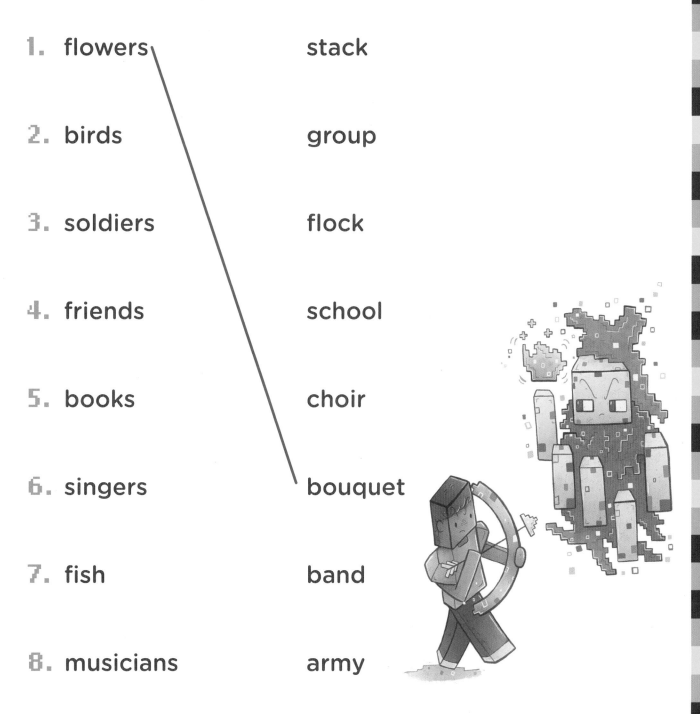

SCIENCE WORD SCRAMBLE

Unscramble the science words below. Use the words in the word box to help you.

observe	effect	roots	solution
~~cause~~	sun	problem	solar

1. secua _____ cause _____

2. rlosa _____

3. feectf _____

4. svoebre _____

5. moplebr _____

6. linsouto _____

7. uns _____

8. storo _____

SORT THE WORDS

Sort the words in the word box into the correct category in the chart.

skeleton	health
sword	create
grow	angry
funny	golden
scary	chop
play	witch

NOUN   VERB   ADJECTIVE

skeleton _____ _____

_____ _____ _____

_____ _____ _____

_____ _____ _____

THE POWER OF PREFIXES

A **prefix** is a letter or group of letters that go in front of a word and change the meaning of the word.

dis-   *means "not"*

over-   *means "too much"*

Fill in the chart by adding the prefix to the root word. Then explain the meaning of the new word.

ROOT WORD	PREFIX	NEW WORD	MEANING
like	dis-	dislike	not like
eat	over-		
agree	dis-		
work	over-		
do	over-		
able	dis-		

SIGHT WORD SEARCH

Sight words are words that appear many times in the books you read. Learn them and reading will be easier! Find the words in the word search puzzle.

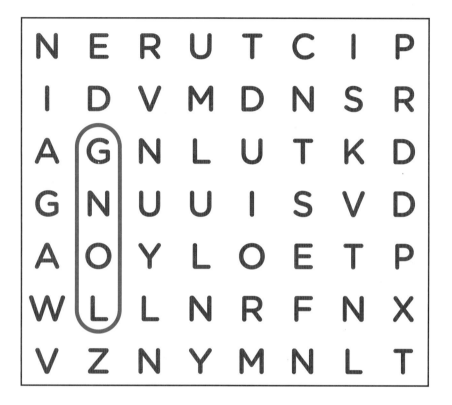

```
N  E  R  U  T  C  I  P
I  D  V  M  D  N  S  R
A (G) N  L  U  T  K  D
G (N) U  U  I  S  V  D
A (O) Y  L  O  E  T  P
W (L) L  N  R  F  N  X
V  Z  N  Y  M  N  L  T
```

~~long~~	must
would	still
again	picture
found	very

CROSSWORD FOR CRAFTERS

Sight words are words that appear many times in the books you read. Learn them and reading will be easier! Use the sight words in the box and the clues to finish the puzzle.

different	turn	another	much
hand	~~want~~	right	year

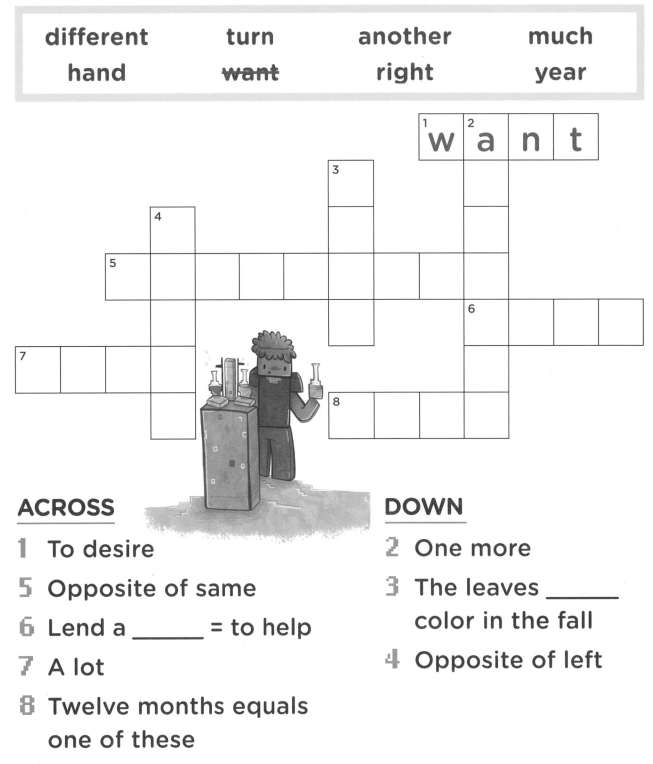

ACROSS

1 To desire

5 Opposite of same

6 Lend a _____ = to help

7 A lot

8 Twelve months equals one of these

DOWN

2 One more

3 The leaves _____ color in the fall

4 Opposite of left

LANGUAGE ARTS WORD SCRAMBLE

Unscramble the language arts words below. Use the words in the word box to help you.

paragraph	publish	sentence	punctuation
~~vowel~~	silent	rhyme	mark

1. lvewo ___vowel___

2. tliesn _____

3. mryhe _____

4. garprapha _____

5. ctonouuapit _____

6. entsecen _____

7. spuilhb _____

8. rakm _____

SUPER SUFFIXES

A **suffix** is a letter or group of letters that go at the end of a word and change the meaning of the word.

-est *means "the most"*

-less *means "without"*

Fill in the chart by adding the suffix to the root word. Then explain the meaning.

ROOT WORD	SUFFIX	NEW WORD	MEANING
end	-less	endless	without end
clean	-est		
fear	-less		
slow	-est		
hope	-less		
small	-est		

SOCIAL STUDIES WORD SCRAMBLE

Unscramble the social studies words below. Use the words in the word box to help you.

desert	~~country~~	fact	change
opinion	holiday	landform	community

1. ryctonu ___country___

2. stered _____

3. inpooni _____

4. cfat _____

5. fmolrdna _____

6. yhoaild _____

7. munmcoyti _____

8. egcahn _____

SIGHT WORD SYNONYMS

Synonyms are words that mean the same thing. Match each **sight word** in the left column with its same meaning in the right column.

1. home 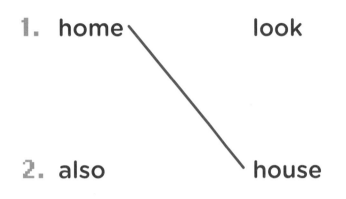 look

2. also house

3. say sound

4. see too

5. noise nice

6. kind tell

COMMONLY CONFUSED WORDS

Some words sound the same but are spelled differently and mean different things. The words in parentheses are often confused for each other. Write the correct word on the line to complete the sentence.

1. ___**Would**___ you play Minecraft with me?
   (would, wood)

2. The spider built a web on the _____
   side of the cave.   *(write, right)*

3. The arrow flew _____ the piglin's head.
   (by, bye)

4. Feed the _____ apple to the horse.
   (red, read)

5. The _____ lives in a hut in the forest.
   (which, witch)

6. We _____ the game!
   (won, one)

7. The iron golem raised _____ fist.
   (its, it's)

FILL-IN-THE-BLANK STORY

Use your own words to complete the Minecraft story.

An Enderman is a _____tall_____ creature. If

you see an Enderman, be very _____ .

It might try to attack you. Do not look it in the

_____ . You can hide inside of a

_____ or behind a _____ .

If you have a weapon like a _____ , you

can destroy it. Endermen

like to _____ a

block in their hands. What

a _____ mob!

VERBS ENDING WITH –Y

When a verb ends in **y**, change the y to **-ied** to make it past tense.

BASE FORM	PAST TENSE
fry	fried
carry	
marry	
ready	
deny	
supply	
bury	

MATCH THE SUBJECT AND VERB

Fill in the chart with the correct form of the verb.

BASE FORM	SHE OR HE	THEY	I	YOU
find	finds	find	find	find
call				
see				
need				
set				

COMPOUND WORDS

Compound words combine two single words into a new word. Combine the two words shown in the chart to make a new word.

book	+	shelf	=	*bookshelf*
day	+	time	=	
air	+	port	=	
with	+	out	=	
sun	+	light	=	
bed	+	room	=	
eye	+	ball	=	

QUESTION WORDS

Use one of the question words to fill in the blank.

Who	What	When	Where	~~How~~

1. **QUESTION:** _____How_____ long does a potion last?
   ANSWER: It lasts about 8 minutes.

2. **QUESTION:** _____ do piglins fear most?
   ANSWER: They fear soul fire.

3. **QUESTION:** _____ was Minecraft released?
   ANSWER: Minecraft was released in 2009.

4. **QUESTION:** _____ do slimes spawn?
   ANSWER: They spawn in the Overworld.

5. **QUESTION:** _____ is Herobrine?
   ANSWER: He is a Minecraft ghost.

Now write your own question about Minecraft using a question word above. Then write the answer.

QUESTION: _____

ANSWER: _____

IRREGULAR PLURAL NOUNS

Match each noun with its irregular plural form.

1. leaf   wolves

2. ox   sheep

3. knife   geese

4. wolf   leaves

5. goose   loaves

6. loaf   knives

7. sheep   lives

8. life   oxen

ANSWER KEY

PAGE 2

PERSON	PLACE	THING
Alex	Overworld	apple
Steve	Nether	flower
villager		emerald
		pickaxe

PAGE 3
1. six
2. two
3. seven
4. three
5. four
6. five

PAGE 4
1. loud
2. fast
3. spotted
4. diamond
5. tamed
6. boss

PAGE 5
1. cute

2–4. Answers will vary but should include one of the three provided synonyms.

Answers will vary but may include huge, enormous, gigantic, massive, or colossal.

PAGE 6
1. Where
2. What
3. How
4. When
5. Why

Answers will vary but should include one of the question words.

PAGE 7

PAGE 8
1. measure
2. weight
3. add
4. sum
5. equal
6. subtract
7. shape
8. length

PAGE 9

ROOT WORD	PREFIX	NEW WORD	MEANING
happy	un-	unhappy	not happy
play	re-	replay	play again
true	un-	untrue	not true
do	re-	redo	do again
lucky	un-	unlucky	not lucky
read	re-	reread	read again

PAGE 10
1. quietly
2. slowly
3. quickly
4. happily
5. loudly
6. gently

PAGE 11
1. hers
2. theirs
3. yours
4. his
5. mine
6. ours

PAGE 12

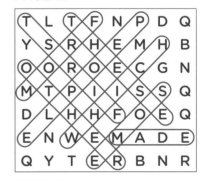

PAGE 13
1. oil
2. moon
3. energy
4. earth
5. plant
6. pattern
7. sound
8. system

PAGE 14

1. baby — babies
2. butterfly — butterflies
3. try — tries
4. city — cities
5. party — parties
6. lily — lilies
7. study — studies

PAGE 15

BASE FORM	PAST TENSE
call	called
teleport	teleported
chase	chased
mine	mined
attack	attacked
plant	planted

PAGE 16

BASE FORM	PAST TENSE
sit	sat
hide	hid
tell	told
sleep	slept
make	made
get	got
fight	fought

PAGE 17

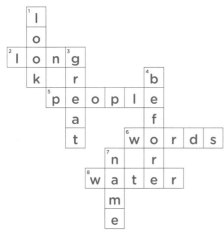

PAGE 18

1. The <u>player</u> spawns the <u>skeleton</u>.
2. In his <u>hand</u> is a <u>pickaxe</u>.
3. The gamer wears (gold) armor.
4. The player has a (diamond) pickaxe.
5. The player |inspects| the spawner cage.
6. The skeleton |looks| scared.
7. Answers will vary.

PAGE 19

COLOR	CLOTHING
blue	pants
orange	shirts
green	shoes
white	coat
purple	scarf

PAGE 20

1. draft
2. period
3. letter
4. sentence
5. capital
6. revise
7. author

PAGE 21

BASE FORM	FUTURE TENSE
see	will see
use	will use
craft	will craft
get	will get
chop	will chop
build	will build

PAGE 22

1. was
2. did
3. had
4. made
5. said
6. were
7. wrote

PAGE 23

1. b
2. a
3. b
4. b
5. a
6. a

PAGE 24

ROOT WORD	PREFIX	NEW WORD	MEANING
joy	-ful	joyful	full of joy
act	-or	actor	a person who acts
fear	-ful	fearful	full of fear
edit	-or	editor	a person who edits
hope	-ful	hopeful	full of hope
sail	-or	sailor	a person who sails

PAGE 25

1. iron
2-6. Answers will vary.

PAGE 26
1. bravely
2. very
3. easily
4. sadly
5. neatly
6. loudly

PAGE 27
1. culture
2. map
3. globe
4. family
5. history
6. value
7. belief
8. symbol

PAGE 28

ANIMAL	NUMBER
dog	three
bat	seven
cat	nine
fish	ten
squid	eight

PAGE 29

PAGE 30

SINGULAR	PLURAL
fence	fences
fox	foxes
ender pearl	ender pearls
block	blocks
llama	llamas
bush	bushes
ladder	ladders
compass	compasses

PAGE 31
1. their
2. two
3. hear
4. your
5. its
6. lets

PAGE 32

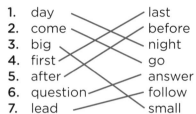

1. day — night
2. come — go
3. big — small
4. first — last
5. after — before
6. question — answer
7. lead — follow

PAGE 33

PRESENT TENSE	PAST TENSE
catch	caught
sleep	slept
begin	began
come	came
say	said
see	saw

PAGE 34
1. Are
2. been
3. buy
4. knew
5. sea
6. great
7. no

PAGE 35
1. zero
2. minus
3. whole
4. graph
5. double
6. value
7. round
8. digit

PAGE 36

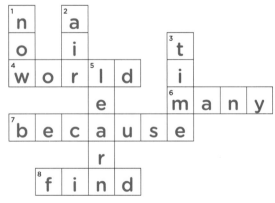

PAGE 37

1. madness
   mad ness
2. undone
   un done
3. timeless
   time less
4. useful
   use ful
5. teacher
   teach er
6. remove
   re move
7. return
   re turn
8. learner
   learn er

PAGE 38

1. help
2. feed
3. lead
4. ship
5. chest
6. see
7. green
8. smart

PAGE 39

BASE FORM	SHE OR HE	THEY	I	YOU
hop	hops	hop	hop	hop
write	writes	write	write	write
help	helps	help	help	help
live	lives	live	live	live
read	reads	read	read	read

PAGE 40

bed	+	time	=	bedtime
row	+	boat	=	rowboat
back	+	pack	=	backpack
bird	+	house	=	birdhouse
note	+	book	=	notebook
book	+	mark	=	bookmark
class	+	room	=	classroom

PAGE 41

1. flowers — bouquet
2. birds — flock
3. soldiers — army
4. friends — group
5. books — stack
6. singers — choir
7. fish — school
8. musicians — band

PAGE 42

1. cause
2. solar
3. effect
4. observe
5. problem
6. solution
7. sun
8. roots

PAGE 43

NOUN	VERB	ADJECTIVE
skeleton	grow	funny
sword	play	scary
health	create	angry
witch	chop	golden

PAGE 44

ROOT WORD	PREFIX	NEW WORD	MEANING
like	dis-	dislike	not like
eat	over-	overeat	eat too much
agree	dis-	disagree	not agree
work	over-	overwork	work too much
do	over-	overdo	do too much
able	dis-	disable	not able

PAGE 45

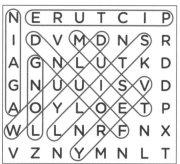

PAGE 46

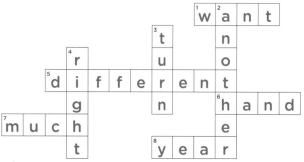

PAGE 47
1. vowel
2. silent
3. rhyme
4. paragraph
5. punctuation
6. sentence
7. publish
8. mark

PAGE 48

ROOT WORD	SUFFIX	NEW WORD	MEANING
end	-less	endless	without end
clean	-est	cleanest	the most clean
fear	-less	fearless	without fear
slow	-est	slowest	the most slow
hope	-less	hopeless	without hope
small	-est	smallest	the most small

PAGE 49
1. country
2. desert
3. opinion
4. fact
5. landform
6. holiday
7. community
8. change

PAGE 50
1. home — too
2. also — nice
3. say — look
4. see — house
5. noise — sound
6. kind — tell

PAGE 51
1. Would
2. right
3. by
4. red
5. witch
6. won
7. its

PAGE 52
1. tall
2-8. Answers will vary.

PAGE 53

BASE FORM	PAST TENSE
fry	fried
carry	carried
marry	married
ready	readied
deny	denied
supply	supplied
bury	buried

PAGE 54

BASE FORM	SHE OR HE	THEY	I	YOU
find	finds	find	find	find
call	calls	call	call	call
see	sees	see	see	see
need	needs	need	need	need
set	sets	set	set	set

PAGE 55

book	+	shelf	=	bookshelf
day	+	time	=	daytime
air	+	port	=	airport
with	+	out	=	without
sun	+	light	=	sunlight
bed	+	room	=	bedroom
eye	+	ball	=	eyeball

PAGE 56
1. How
2. What
3. When
4. Where
5. Who
Answers will vary.

PAGE 57

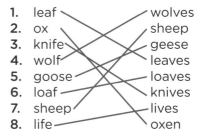

1. leaf — leaves
2. ox — oxen
3. knife — knives
4. wolf — wolves
5. goose — geese
6. loaf — loaves
7. sheep — sheep
8. life — lives